LOVE BETWEEN
THE PAGES

By
Connie Faye Thamert

With
Stephen A. White

I dedicate this book to my husband, my lover, my best friend, and my soulmate, John Anthony Rohanna, and to those who wonder if there is love somewhere out there… there is!

Table of Contents

FOREWORD ... Page 5

INTRODUCTION ... Page 6

CHAPTER 1. Florida... Page 8

CHAPTER 2. What Just Happened? ... Page 18

CHAPTER 3. Getting to Know You... Page 25

CHAPTER 4. "Hello, John; Hello, Connie" ... Page 35

CHAPTER 5. Getting Together—Part I ... Page 42

CHAPTER 6. Marriage on the Rocks ... Page 56

CHAPTER 7. Getting Together—Part II ... Page 61

CHAPTER 8. Love *After* the Pages ... Page 76

CHAPTER 9. One Big Happy Family ... Page 87

CHAPTER 10. Final Thoughts ... Page 103

FOREWORD -- *Stephen A. White*

On December 21, 2020, I received an email from a woman in Rochester, Minnesota.

I have a story I need to get down in some form- I do not want to leave here without telling it. I would like to tell you about it, if that is possible.

I have over 300 letters from 1987- my letters and his letters- I am working on them to make them legible (ink fades)- it somehow is a slice of life that I want to preserve, even if it just for myself. I need help!

I have to decide if I want to share this story or is it enough to know that I was the luckiest woman in the world?-- Connie

I was hooked—who writes 300 love letters? And how did this happen over 1300 miles from each other, while both parties were still married with children? I needed to find out. And, thankfully, Connie *did* want to share the story.

Over the course of six months, I interviewed Connie Thamert about her relationship with John Rohanna, and read some of the letters they wrote to each other. Through those letters, even a blind man could see how much in love they were with each other, and why they were meant to be together.

And why their story had to be told.

INTRODUCTION – *Connie Thamert*

☐ I went into the basement storage room one day, moved a few Christmas ornament boxes, some old children's toys, and a few other items, and found the box that was labeled *"Letters"*.

I hadn't looked in the box for over 30 years and was surprised that besides all the letters (still in their envelopes) was the yellow ribbon that had been tied around a tree for John's arrival.

Grabbing what I could, I went upstairs and started to sort through the letters and reread them. We both had saved the other's letters, and they told a story of our accidental meeting and our amazement at what had happened to us from that moment on. We were just two ordinary people from different parts of the country, that had stumbled across each other and each felt we had "come home."

We felt as if we had known each other for a long, long time. As I began to read the letters and lose myself in our mutual amazement, I also began to wonder if there was a way to tell our story. Could the letters be used to tell it? It certainly was not practical to publish all the letters (some were 9-12 pages long), but there were excerpts that could illustrate how this happened and what we were feeling on our "ride downstream."

Writing letters is somewhat of a "lost art." In the time before cell phones, texting, and even emails, our letter-writing expressed our thoughts and emotions in ways that even surprised us. We learned about each other and also learned about ourselves. We wondered what was happening and discovered it was love and was meant to be. More importantly, we discovered how to GIVE love to each other.

The letters are our legacy to love; a rare thing we found from page to page.

I hope you enjoy the journey.

Connie F. Thamert

John & Connie... 1987

Chapter 1

Florida

Sunday, March 15, 1987

I am sitting in a Denny's in Kissimmee, Florida at 3:00am. The coffee is weak and my eggs are getting cold, but I really don't care. I am there with my best friend, Marianne, and we had travelled from a very snowy Minnesota to a very warm Central Florida, along with Marianne's parents, to enjoy some time at Disney World. But Marianne isn't the only person at the table. John Rohanna is sitting across from me, and he is the reason I could care less about cold eggs and weak coffee.

I had met John the night before at a club called Little Darlin's Rock 'N Roll Palace. It was one of those retro clubs with a façade that resembled a giant jukebox. Inside there was a loft where you could sit and look down at the band (naturally playing '50s tunes—The Diamonds, The Platters, Buddy Holly), a dance floor and some tables. John was there with two of his friends—Bill and Lenny—and they were visiting Disney World with their families. We noticed them looking at our table

(Marianne was 12 years my junior) and they eventually sent beers over.

Okay, maybe we should take a little pause here and give some more perspective of the time and place.

I wasn't some giddy teenager sitting in a nightclub looking to have a wild night out, flirting with guys and collecting free drinks. When the waitress brought over those beers I was a 44-year old nurse from Rochester, Minnesota, working on the cardiac floor at the Mayo Clinic. I was also married for almost 22 years and the mother of three beautiful children; Rachel, Michael and Annie.

I met my husband, Jack, in a bar in 1963 while I was enrolled at Mankato State University in Mankato, Minnesota. I was out with some girlfriends and started talking to these two guys. One of the guys, Jack, was just back from the Navy. I learned from our conversation that he was a big college wrestler. In fact, he was a national champ in college in 1958. We clicked, fell in love, and got married in July of 1965.

Like most marriages, the honeymoon seemed to last forever, until it didn't. Eventually our marriage took on what I would best describe as a neutral tone. Things started to taper off emotionally and physically. We would still be occasionally intimate, but it usually started with Jack out for a night with his buddies and a nudge when he crawled into bed. It was almost like living with your brother, although that may sound a little creepy. We never got to the point where we really hated each other, or even disliked each other. But between raising children and taking care of Jack and the house, I sometimes felt more like a caregiver than a wife. I felt like I was in a rut the size of the Grand Canyon.

When Marianne, a fellow soccer mom, invited me to go to Disney World with her and her parents, I jumped at the chance. It was not only because I had never been there before, or because there was quite likely two feet of snow on the ground outside my house, but because it was a chance to get away and breathe. When I told Jack I was heading off to Disney World his reaction was no reaction. That's just the way he was. His mantra was always you do your thing and I'll do mine. That way of thinking sort of defined our marriage in the last few years.

Jack was never outright mean, but he could land a zinger or two. For instance, I was very happy working as a nurse in a nursing home, but Jack made me feel like I should apologize for not being a "real" nurse in a hospital; like I was inadequate. But I liked being a nurse in a nursing home. I think there's a definite need for that. And I loved those elderly people. But Jack argued that I could make much more money at the Mayo Clinic, so that is where I ended up. It eventually turned out for the best—I loved my job—but there was never the feeling that it was *my* decision.

So it was off to the Land of the Mouse. You have to remember that the Disney World of 1987 is very different than the Disney World of today. Back then there were only two parks; the Magic Kingdom and Epcot. The only hotels on the property were the Polynesian and the Contemporary, and even back then they were a little too expensive for our tastes, so we stayed at a hotel outside of the parks. Our trip was planned for a Friday through Tuesday, so we had a four-day pass. On Sunday, after a day at the park, Marianne suggested that we should go to this club in Kissimmee that played all oldies music and grab a beer or two. Sounded like fun.

When we got to the club it was already pretty crowded. There was a $10 cover charge, which was probably the most I'd ever paid for a cover charge in my life. We could hear the music from the outside. When we entered, we walked up the stairs and found a table looking down at the dance floor. Eventually we found a table downstairs and had more drinks. That's when the beers showed up at our table, courtesy of Bill, Lenny and John. Eventually the three of them came over to our table and we just started chatting. I recall Bill was criticizing Marianne's choice of footwear (she was in full flirt mode). Bill told her that her choice of sandals was all wrong for walking around Disney World. Lenny didn't say much of anything; probably the quiet type. John was also very quiet, not because he was the silent type but because it was very apparent he had a few drinks and looked like he needed a good night's sleep. He was 48-years old, just under six feet, medium build and very good looking. He wore khaki pants, a yellow shirt and a blue cardigan sweater. And he had a tan Irish L. L. Bean scally cap on his head, pulled slightly down over his eyes. He looked really tired.

Attempting to make some conversation, I asked him his name. He said it was Joe O'Hara. I don't know why he said that because it wasn't believable. So I asked Bill, and he said his friend's name was John. After awhile John (not Joe) and I started to get along very well, even to the point of dancing, most likely to a Little Richard tune (*Wop-bop-a-loom-a-boom-bam-boom!*). I had a great time.

Around 1:00am things were starting to wind down at the club. The band had packed up and left and the waitresses were starting to clear tables, I was worried that the night was ending too soon, but Lenny solved that problem by suggesting we all head off to the local Denny's and grab some late-night breakfast. The guys left the club first, and when Marianne and I walked out John was leaning against one of the posts on the front of the club in his blue cardigan. Bill and Lenny were already in a car, so John decided he would drive over with us in Marianne's car. John wanted me to sit in the back seat with him. I was shocked. In the first place I wouldn't do that to a friend. And in the second place, I just wouldn't do that with someone I had just met. So John sat in the back, and maybe as a compromise, he held my hand over the seat the entire way to Denny's.

We all ordered breakfast but I didn't eat a lot as I was totally enthralled in my conversation with John. We talked of many things; life, horse racing (he was part owner in a couple of racehorses), cars, his experiences in the Navy when he was 17. He loved being in the Navy, calling it some of the best years of his life. He was on a carrier, the U.S.S. Saratoga and he loved being out on the ocean. He said he could stand and look at the ocean for hours.

I told him about my experiences as a nurse, my dad's death in 1978, my brother's death in 1968, my brother's struggle with alcoholism, the fact that I was 10 years younger than my brother, how I gave a friend a bloody nose when she said something bad about my brother. John spoke so proudly of his Irish heritage and of growing up in the Dorchester section of Boston. He made it sound so special. I spoke of my patients and their vulnerability, their trust and faith. He wasn't all that convinced that there is goodness in people.

He told me several times that he would see me again. He was so sure of that. He told me he was married twice, once when he was quite young, and both women had the same last names, although they were not related. I told John I was married to a man also named John, but he went by Jack and he was a nice guy. Marianne agreed that he was a nice guy. John insisted that we would meet again and even picked the date: January 8, 1988. And just to be "annoying," he kept putting his hat on me, then taking it off, putting it on. He also kept putting out my cigarettes, saying, "You don't need those." It seemed he had just quit smoking earlier that year. I have no recollection of what anyone else was saying. It felt like it was just John and I sitting in that restaurant.

Just before 4:00am it was decided that we should be heading out, which made me sad; I felt like I had connected with my soul mate. But there were other lives we had to return to. Standing outside the restaurant John insisted that he was going to see me again. I said, "How do you figure that, you know, it's just an accident that we met?" Then he kissed me. It wasn't anything aggressive, like heavy making out. It was just the nicest kiss, and then he leaned back and he said, "Wow." I asked him where were we going to meet and he said, "We'll go to Rome. Rome, New York. Or to Paris, Texas." We both laughed at that. He asked me for my address so he could write me and, of course, I couldn't give him my home address for obvious reasons.

He gave me his business card for his company, Integrity Auto Sales, and I wrote Marianne's address on the back. Then we went our separate ways, leaving me thinking to myself, "Would he really write to me?"

We had a few last days at Disney World before heading back to the frozen north, and trying as hard as I could, I never saw John among the hundreds of thousands of people in the park. John Rohanna was the proverbial needle in a haystack. Plus, it suddenly occurred to me; I didn't have his address or phone! Only the name of the company.

On Tuesday, March 17, we got ready to head home. But there was something that happened as I got on the plane that affected me personally. There was some delay with the flight and we were sitting on the tarmac, which gave me ample time to go to the bathroom. When I returned to my seat Marianne was listening to music on her headphones. Suddenly she handed me the earphones and said, "You gotta listen to this." I put on the headphones and it was Linda Ronstadt singing, "Somewhere Out There" from the animated movie, *An American Tail.* Right away the lyrics struck me because they were talking about two people being separated but still sleeping under the same big sky. It almost felt like John was making a connection to me through the song.

As we lifted off, I sat in my seat and looked out the window as Disney World faded away beneath the clouds. And I thought of John, and of the hours we spent connecting. He said he would write, but would he. *Should he?* After all, we were both married. Still, I felt he would keep his promise. I hoped he would.

As the plane rose higher, I remember thinking it was very likely snowing, cold and windy in Rochester, Minnesota. But it didn't matter; my heart was on fire 30,000-feet over Florida.

Chapter 2

What Just Happened?

I had a lot of time to think about the events in Florida. After all, that's what happens when your plane is delayed leaving Tampa Airport, which causes you to arrive late in Minneapolis-St. Paul, which causes you to miss your connecting flight to Rochester, Minnesota. While we waited over three hours to catch the next 40-minute flight to Rochester, Marianne and I killed time at the bar. Although she would never admit it (years later she would comment that at that time it was like "I wasn't really there."), I am guessing that my lack of conversation had a lot to do with what had just transpired in Orlando. John was on my mind, as was the question; "Where was he 25 years ago?"

After arriving home and handing off to the kids all the goodies that I had brought back from Disney World (including plastic swords that almost got me banned from the flight), I began to realize that even if nothing came out of the encounter (a sad thought) that the time I spent with John had instilled a new-found confidence in me, something that had been sorely lacking for the past 25 years. I had always put myself on the back burner. It was all about the kids and Jack's job, to the point that I had become what no person wants to be; an afterthought. But talking with John and opening up to him, knowing that he was actually *listening to me*, and that I wasn't just background noise in my own house, was invigorating. Still, it wasn't hard to be a little skeptical about the whole thing; maybe women are wired that way. Why would he make me feel that way? I didn't know what to think. But there was no denying the facts; John Rohanna had refueled my sense of confidence. Maybe I was important after all.

Life suddenly seemed brighter to me, more vibrant. It's hard to say if Jack and the kids noticed the changes, but I certainly did. I know I felt different to myself. I felt empowered. I made the decision to improve my wardrobe and make myself more attractive. Maybe even spice up life in the bedroom a little in order to try to put some juice into the marriage and see what would happen. But I also asked myself; am I "juicing" to invigorate my marriage, or to prove to myself (and Jack) that I can?

Still, while I was undergoing this personal metamorphosis, my mind never strayed far from thoughts of John. I felt the need to connect, and the first thing was to actually figure out where he was and how I could reconnect, should the time be right.

This is what I knew, and it was sadly very little. I had a name and the name of the company that he owned, and a pretty good idea about the geographic location. I had written Marianne's home address on the back of his business card then handed it back to him without asking the most basic question; "Could I have your address?" That was a basic "duh" moment, but there was no use crying over spilled milk. At least I remembered the name of his company; Integrity Auto Sales. So how did one stalk in a pre-Google age? Easy; the *Yellow Pages*. And for those younger folks who don't know what the *Yellow Pages* are, feel free to Google it.

I headed down to the local public library and rifled through the Boston-area *Yellow Pages*, but had no luck. Who doesn't put their business in the *Yellow Pages?* Then I tried the *White Pages* and hit pay dirt. Looking at the address, it felt like my first real reconnection since getting off the plane. I jotted the address and phone number down (although I was too shy to actually call) without even bothering to check further for a home address since I knew I would never be sending a letter to it.

After about a week since leaving Florida, I have to admit I was starting to have my doubts about where this was going to go, and if there was even a "this" to worry about. He kept saying that night in Orlando that he was going to write to me the night he got home. But I wasn't so certain; do men even write letters? Perhaps I would have to make the first move. So I made the bold decision to send him a greeting card. Choosing the card resulted in a lot of soul-searching for just the right card, one that would resonate with him and speak to what we shared. And since he was Irish, and looked dashing in his scally cap, the decision was an easy one; a St. Patrick's Day card, albeit a belated one.

Even as I perused the aisles of Hunt's Drug & Gift Shop looking for leftover St. Patrick's Day cards in the racks, I still wasn't sure if I should send one, or if it was the right thing to do. But ultimately my wish to reconnect with John won the day. Still, buying the card was only half the battle. Once I bought it, the question of what to write on it was a whole different ballgame. I eventually settled on a greeting card that had a brandy snifter glass tipped on its side, with green M&M's spilling out. Inside the message read: "I'm saving the green one's for you." Little did I know at the time that green M&M's are considered an aphrodisiac (or maybe subliminally I did know that).

The card now safely in my possession, I then decided it was unfair to make Marianne my messenger girl, and although I knew she would never read any letter that John sent her way (if he *did* send one), I decided it would make more sense to purchase a post office box.

But before we actually discuss purchasing a post office box, it's important to fully understand that back in 1987 Rochester was a relatively small city. I'm not talking Mayberry small, but at perhaps a little over 75,000 people it wasn't actually downtown Chicago, or even Duluth. The city had an intimate feel, therefore it always seemed like everyone knew everyone else. So discretion was the key. When I entered the post office on Valleyhigh Drive, I made sure there wasn't anyone I recognized among the people waiting to mail letters or pick up parcels. When I finally got to the window, I said softly (but loud enough for the worker to hear me) that I wanted to purchase a post office box. Well, discretion went out the window when the guy taking my order yelled out loud enough for the folks in the Twin Cities to hear it; "Hey, Charlie, this lady over here wants to open a post office box, can you help her?" And I thought, "Oh my God!" I looked around to see if I knew anybody because doesn't every housewife have a secret post office box?

Eventually I was given box number 6961, and set about making out the card. Sitting on my deck (the kids were at school and Jack at work), I struggled with what to write. After some serious soul-searching I proceeded to write:

You are a charming and interesting person and I enjoyed talking with you. Connie

Okay, short and sweet. Not exactly a love sonnet, but I felt it sufficient enough to test the waters. I also enclosed a little card with a shamrock on it and wrote down my P.O. Box address. And on March 24th, I dropped it in the mail, figuring that the way the post office worked he'd probably get it about four days later. Then what? Would he toss it in the trash, or would he respond? Every day I would journey down to the post office and stare through the little glass window of my post office box. Nothing.

Then one day persistence paid off. I walked into the post office, looked in the box, and lo and behold, there was an envelope sitting in it. Since only John had my P.O. Box number, it wasn't hard to deduce it was from him. I felt myself shaking as I inserted the key and opened the box. I was so excited as I took out the letter, not believing that he actually wrote back to me! I thought I was going to cry.

Once again making sure there was no one who knew me, I carried the letter back to my used Chevy station wagon. I opened it, hands shaking, and unfolded the pages. It was dated March 31, 1987, and it only took the first few lines to make my heart sing:

Dear Connie, I received your note and was surprised to hear from you (not really, I guess). This is the 5th or 6th time I tried to write this letter, all before I received your note, which gave me the additional push I needed to write you without feeling like a total fool...

Chapter 3

Getting to Know You

I don't know how many times I read that first letter from John. Twice, three times maybe? I'm not really sure. Sitting in my car in the post office parking lot, I absorbed each word like a thirsty sponge.

> ***It is much easier to talk about writing as it is to do the actual writing (so I will just write as if I'm talking to you)***

It was as if he were sitting here in the car beside me, I thought to myself. John's first letter was all about trying to get to know me better, discovering things we didn't have the chance to touch upon with our all-too-brief Florida get-together. He talked about taking a crash course on Rochester, Minnesota, beyond just the Mayo Clinic. He asked about the weather in April *("Is it Spring yet")*. But I could tell, as if I were with him, that he was having difficulty in knowing what to write.

I'm having a hard time saying what I'm trying to say, and I don't even know what that is. I hope to hear from you again, but if you choose not to, I would understand why.

Okay, that's *definitely* not going to be the case. By the time I put John's letter in my backpack, I was already thinking of my response. I wanted to get a letter off as quickly as I could.

The next day I had the house to myself. The kids were off doing their thing and Jack was at work. As I sat at the kitchen table, pen in hand, I thought about what to say. I felt like I was at the beginning of some serious literary foreplay as we were exploring each other's little corner of the world. Now on my second cup of coffee, I began to write:

Dear John, it was really nice to hear from you. Actually, that is an understatement if I've ever made one. It was much more than nice—it was vital, I've been trying to figure out what happened in Orlando on the Ides of March. This person from Mass. and this person from Minn. accidentally came together and something happened. I felt like I've known you, or should have known you, for some time. Where were you 25 years ago?

From there I tried to fill in some of the blanks on John Rohanna; what's Boston's weather like, tell me about the Red

Sox, what's your middle name? I asked about his horses and what his favorite Irish songs were (also requesting a tape). When was his birthday? And I also made it a point to mention the song "Somewhere Out There," as I felt the lyrics mirrored what was happening in our respective lives. That two people could be so far apart and yet so close together:

Somewhere out there
Beneath the pale moonlight
Someone's thinking of me
And loving me tonight

Somewhere out there
Someone's saying a prayer
That we'll find one another
In that big somewhere out there

And even though I know how very far apart we are
It helps to think we might be wishing on the same bright star
And when the night wind starts to sing a lonesome lullaby
It helps to think we're sleeping underneath the same big sky

Somewhere out there
If love can see us through
Then we'll be together

Somewhere out there
Out where dreams come true

By putting that letter in the mail shortly after writing it, as a response to John's initial correspondence, little did I know that I was about to set off a postal chain reaction that would result in nearly 20 letters exchanged between us in April alone, and over 300 handwritten letters by the end of February 1988 (totaling over a hand-cramping 2,000 pages). But as I said in one of my letters, the die had been cast. Now I had to be cautious that the die didn't get caught.

John's next letter arrived about a week after I put mine in the mailbox. Right away he brightened my day by telling me he read my last letter 20 times (Who does that?). We were still in the "courting" stages as he was using the *Encyclopedia Americana* to look up things about Minnesota and watching the Weather Channel to see what things were like in Minnesota, as well as following the Minnesota North Stars and Minnesota Twins in the newspaper box scores. Or, as he wrote:

Connie,

I'm not trying to bore you with the sports pages, but to show you the impact you have made upon me. I don't know exactly where I was 25 years ago. But I do know I was in the right place on March 15 for about four hours.

John

John went on to promise to send me tapes of his favorite Irish music, and talked a bit about his love of horse racing. And as he started to wrap up his letter, this is what caught me squarely in the heart:

Connie,

I don't know if you believe in fate. But as a gambler, I do. But I am confused. Why, after only one night of talking with someone, do I feel so confused?

John

As I put the letter back in its envelope and tucked it in my backpack for safekeeping, I asked myself the same question.

On the night of April 16, 1987, I found I had trouble falling asleep. It was around 4:00am. I got up and went into the dining room, near the patio sliding glass door, as far away from the bedroom as I could get so I took the opportunity to write a short letter to John. I never realized at the time that that *short letter* would turn out to be 11 pages long. John had used the term "ragtime" when describing things that were sentimental feelings that touched so close to the heart. Well, at 11 pages, this letter was ragtime on steroids. I wrote for two hours and went back to bed at 6:00am. When I awoke at 7:00am, I reread what I had written, but didn't change anything. As a matter of fact, I had some severe doubts as to whether or not I should send it. But I eventually did.

Much of the letter started with a description of what Rochester, Minnesota was like, as if he had requested literature from a travel agent. I talked about the Mayo Clinic and IBM, two major employers in the region. The doctors I liked and those I could do without. I talked about Canadian geese pooping on people's lawns (very romantic) and how my kids did at soccer. John got introduced to my card-playing mother and educated by me on the history of thoroughbred horses (which had nothing to do with Minnesota). I was on a roll and basically throwing the proverbial kitchen sink into my letter. But even a ragtime letter had to end somewhere.

John,

I don't know why I'm telling you all this. I hope you don't think I'm crazy. It's like I want you to know all about me. I guess I should close this epic. I really am going to overwhelm you, I'm afraid, but what the hell! I think of you often. Actually, I've been thinking of you too much!

Connie

Hoping that I didn't scare him off with my long, rambling letter, my fears were alleviated when another letter showed up in my post office box (I've been at the post office so much in April I'm surprised they didn't charge me for loitering). The letter was dated April 18, 1987.

Dear Connie.

Received your letter today and I was like a kid at Xmas. You know, excited about opening it. My hands trembled. Sometimes I can't believe the emotions that I feel, like disappointment when the mail comes and I haven't heard from you. Then, exhilaration when I have. I expect to hear twinkling music in the background and Rod Serling's voice saying, "Tonight's episode of The Twilight Zone is entitled "Fours Hours in Orlando." It's where a girl from Olmsted County, Minnesota and a boy from Boston meet for four

hours and feel like they've know each other for all their lives."
It can't be real—But it is!

In this letter John went on to speak about his family. Much as I had about my own in the previous letter. We were definitely getting to know a lot about each other.

We wrote back and forth with great frequency. I was never sure where John wrote his letters, as he was in the same marital situation as I was. Fortunately, working the overnight shift at the nurse's station in the hospital, there was great opportunity to write letters. Occasionally, one of the nurses would see me scribbling away and ask what I was writing. With a smile I would simply reply, "My memoirs."

One night, when things were particularly quiet on the floor, I took the opportunity to write to John about how what I was feeling swelling inside me. I'm glad there wasn't a patient in some room pushing a call button like crazy, as I was laser-focused on what I had to say.

Dear John, I don't care if this is ragtime, I just read your last letter for about the seventh time and you are a lovely,

32

lovely person. I don't care how strange it was that we met. I'm just so glad we did. You touched a chord somewhere deeply buried inside me. It is the most wonderful feeling and I only wish everyone in the world had a chance to feel that way before they die. If I never have anything else, besides our chance meeting, your letters and your warm thoughts, I will still be very happy.

On the night of April 28, 1987, I finally got up the courage to call his office. He wasn't there of course, but I just loved hearing the sound of his voice; *"Have a good one."*

April finally came to a close. It had been a whirlwind month of back and forth letters and, in many ways, living two separate lives. It was also around the time John had to travel up to Pittsburgh, New Hampshire, a small town just a few miles from the Canadian border. He had to attend an automobile auction. In the letter he wrote me, he described traveling north in heavy wet snow, with very poor visibility, Sadly, he was still to find a tape of "Somewhere Out There" to enjoy on the long trip to New Hampshire. But, lo and behold, on the way up he ventured into a small store and there was the tape! He also said he took some of our letters to read while killing some time. One night he ventured down to sit along the banks of the Connecticut Lakes and play the song for the first time. And as he did he saw two loons swimming on the lake, their cry making what John described as "one of the most beautiful sounds in the world." His reaction to the song touched my soul.

Connie,

The words knocked me over. Nothing has ever moved me as that song did at that moment. The words are so beautiful (like Connie). It has to be fate. Is this real.. is this really happening to us? I am emotionally drained.

Thinking of you always, John

And then he wrote a little P.S. at the bottom of the letter, and our world changed forever.

You know I have fallen in love with you, don't you?

Chapter 4

"Hello, John? Hello, Connie?"

May of 1987 became a watershed month that crystallized into a movement that changes our lives. There seemed to be no stopping events that made our world tip sideways.

It seemed like every day I was either writing a letter to John or reading one from him. And it's no wonder since we wrote over 30 letters that month. And our letters became more and more personal and revealing of our deep feelings for each other. After he wrote me about seeing the loons in New Hampshire, and listening to what would be "our song," I wrote:

John,

I am sitting in my car at the post office and I have chills running down both arms and across my back. Both of us have been afraid to say the word love. I think we both know that we must see each other again. I am only a little scared that we won't be able to stand each other. I am not talking about wrenching our lives completely apart. I am only hoping to share whatever this is as often as we can manage it. I have never felt more cared about. I'd like to see you again, John.

Connie

John's response came a few days later.

Connie,

How close our thoughts run. It doesn't surprise me anymore. Of course I want to see you. I've gone over every possible scenario in my mind of what this could eventually bring. We will take what happiness we can gather somewhere in the world that belongs to only you and I. I have fallen in love with the person who writes/says these beautiful letters, who makes me feel important, who shares her feelings with me, who is the kindest, most considerate person I've ever met. I am the luckiest man alive.

John

Although our conversation in the letters was steering towards a rendezvous, it was apparent that we were missing a step in our relationship. In one correspondence John mentioned to me that he dreamed he called me. And at one point he said he almost tried calling me at the hospital. He then asked if we can arrange a call. It was a Saturday and I had written to John that the best time to call me would be Monday to Thursday, around

10:00am Massachusetts time. I am usually home in the morning and nobody else is home; the kids are at school and Jack is off doing his thing.

While this was all going on, good old Marianne stopped by on that same Saturday afternoon. She was aware of what was transpiring between John and me and her good-natured frustration came through loud and clear—"Why don't you just call him?" Good old Marianne.

About 2:00 that afternoon, the house was empty and I dialed John's number at the auto dealer. It seemed like a good time to do it because Saturday was always a good day to sell cars, so I felt pretty confident he would be there. After several rings he answered and it was so wonderful to hear his actual voice since that first night in Orlando some six weeks ago. Even though we had planned to talk initially on Tuesday, I could tell he was surprised, and a little tongued-tied, as was I. Our conversation had what could best be described as an auspicious start.

"John? " "Connie?" "John?" "Connie?"

Okay, it isn't exactly Shakespeare, but more beautiful words had never been spoken. It felt like the world just tipped sideways once again. We talked for a little over 15 minutes and what's funny is neither of us can really remember what we said to each other. The moment felt almost surreal.

In a letter, John would reveal that he felt like a clod with that initial phone call, that perhaps he said the wrongs things, or maybe didn't say enough. I told him not to worry.

John,

Don't ever worry that you could say the wrong things. I love your voice, your accent, your turn of a phrase. Remember the power you have with your sincerity. When we get the chance let's toast to Orlando, L'il Darlin's, New Hampshire, snow storms, loons, lovely music and high-pressure areas. Maybe we can erase some regrets.

Connie

John mentioned that he got so shook up about my calling him out of the blue that he went to visit his parents and he's there until about 4:30 in the morning. Then he drives into downtown Boston and the city streets are lonely and dark because it's a Sunday morning. And he thinks of the Kris Kristofferson song "Sunday Morning Coming Down." By then it's around 8:30 in the morning and he decides to stop by his office and sees the lights blinking on the answering machine. I had called him back and said, "Hi, John." And in a letter he said he was so relieved that he hadn't made a fool of himself on our call the day before. He said never had two words meant so much. It was then that he changed the message on his answering machine to: "You've reached Minnesota or The Twilight Zone."

Connie,

You threw me for a loop with your call. Usually I feel I have a situation under control, except yesterday afternoon. I didn't say what I wanted to say but it meant so much to hear your voice. I feel like I clodded my way through the conversation. I spent last night thinking about that clumsy conversation, that I might have said something to turn you off. But I was in a very emotional state. I guess maybe I'm just an insecure person who needs constant reassurance. Connie, I feel so vulnerable. I think you have looked inside me as no one else has ever done before. My heart and soul are in your hands. By the way, I love your voice. My heart and soul are always in your care.

John

Our relationship had now progressed to the next level thanks to good old Marianne and good old Alexander Graham Bell. We would talk many times on the phone. The calls took place in his office and either at my house or at a phone booth. A question could arise if I was taking a chance sending and receiving calls on my house phone. Wouldn't Jack see the phone bill and question all the "617" calls? That thought never really occurred to me, as I was safe in the knowledge that I was handling paying all the bills. Still many of our calls took place in a cozy little telephone booth in the lobby of St. Mary's Hospital downtown. They were wooden booths and they smelled good and I spent a lot of time in them. To keep from having to constantly pump change into the phone for a long-distance call, I would call John's office and let it ring twice and then hang up. He would call me back if he was available.

It all came down to knowing what I could do and what I couldn't do, or when I couldn't do it. Many nights I put dinner on the table and said I had a meeting at work. Nobody questioned it. I'd go into St Mary's lobby and make my calls, starting with a few each week and then five or six.

People might ask did we feel guilty with what was going on between us, which John addressed in one of his letters.

Connie,

One question we never addressed is, "Are we doing something wrong?" Well, I know other people would say we are. But honestly, Connie, I don't feel we are. I feel we are definitely right for each other in our own little world and I have no guilty feelings at all. It all goes back to the rules of the ride downstream (please always hold my hand), one day at a time, one letter at a time, one meeting at a time, but NEVER any regrets. The only regrets are for things we've never done, not things we will do.

We have no more questions to ask until August 9th.

Love you always, John

August 9, 1987. That was the day John and I chose to take that next leap of faith and meet for the first time since that uneaten breakfast at Denny's in Orlando in the middle of March. This carousel we were both riding was starting to spin faster and faster since the first day we met, and all we could do was hold on for a few more months.

Chapter 5

Getting Together in Minnesota

From April through July 1987, John and I wrote nearly 150 letters to each other, and engaged in at least a couple of dozen phone calls, but it was all really just foreplay leading up to our inevitable rendezvous. Even the best built dams can only hold so much water.

The seed for our get-together was planted in a letter John composed to me on May 8, 1987, in which he wrote:

My Gentle Connie,

All we have to do is figure out where and when. New England, Minnesota, or somewhere in between? I don't care where or when. Next month? Next summer? Next fall? As long as we do it. Now comes the hard part- the wondering- the "What Ifs." What if she has second thoughts, or changes her mind, or doesn't like me? All these things will cross my mind, Gentle Connie. Don't worry, nothing will change my mind.

Love John

I knew in my heart of hearts I wanted this to happen; that it had to happen. I took the initiative.

Hello My Dear, Sweet John,

Why don't you check on August 10th? There is soccer camp that week and it might work out. I could stay Mon and Tues nights, and say I am going to be shopping and visiting some friends. See if the date would work out for you. You could fly back anytime Wed. (I don't like to think of that already). You spoke of "What if's"- don't worry- I think we will be like old friends.

Thinking of you always,

Love Connie

I was fully aware that I had just exposed myself completely and, in some ways, the status of my marriage to Jack. I was never unhappily married, but I was probably never that thrillingly married either. I knew John and I had to see each other again. Still, I was a little nervous that the magic wouldn't still be there, or that I would scare him off. But that didn't deter me.

After doing some research, I decided the best spot would be the Embassy Suites at the airport in Bloomington, Minnesota, about 80 miles from Rochester; a 90-minute drive. I let John know.

Dear John,

I think the Embassy Suites near the Minneapolis airport may be ok for the first time. Minneapolis is a nice city but mostly I think we need to see each other, laugh with each other, talk with each other, touch each other, share with each other, and love each other (uh-oh, did the sky fall in when I said that?). If you want to change it, I'll come there, if you like. Oh, John, it's almost three months away and I sort of get a weak feeling along with Sweet Pain when I think of it.

Thinking of you,

Love Connie

I told John that I'd meet him at the gate, but if I was late arriving for any reason, I'd meet him in the main terminal, at the bar. We had also made the decision to change the date of our rendezvous to August 9th, as it worked out better for both our situations. Still, there seemed to be that slight undercurrent of doubt running through our letters.

Hi Sweet and Gentle Connie Faye,

Do you get nervous thinking about 8/9? I can't wait but sometimes all these "what if's" come sneaking up. And I start to get a little afraid (of what, I don't know OR do I?) Your letters and phone calls are reassuring so then I hope all will go all right. I want to see you so badly, just to look into your beautiful eyes, to hold your hands, to talk to you.

Connie, if you are having 2nd thoughts about 8/9, just let me know, dearest. I would understand. I know we think a lot about our situation- so if you want to rethink things, I understand but please let me know beforehand. I wouldn't want to wait in Minneapolis for someone who never shows. (I don't know why I wrote that- I know you wouldn't do that.) By the way, I'm NOT having second thoughts.

Love you, John

I responded quickly, trying to alleviate any doubts that might cause our ships to go off course on this journey I knew had to happen.

Dearest John,

If, for some reason, I am late getting to the airport on 8/9, I will meet you at the cocktail lounge in the main terminal. I won't be late if I can help it. I don't want to miss a minute of being with you, you know that, don't you?

For some reason, I feel I know our time together will be the MOST enjoyable, joyous, relaxed time of our lives- I know that like I know my name is Connie Faye. We are friends, dear—if we are more than friends, so be it.

John, I will not reconsider- or, if you'd rather, I have thought everything over and over (what you might call reconsidering) and I still want to meet you, see you again, talk to you, listen to you, hold your hand for real, kiss you, walk with you in a park or anywhere- just be with you. But I won't change my mind about 8/9, OK? Whatever else happens is supposed to be- just as this much was supposed to be.

Love Connie

We wrote back and forth quite a few times from that point up until that glorious day in August when John's plane from Boston taxied on the Minneapolis runway. I could feel myself tingling with excitement.

When John's plane disembarked I was there at the gate to meet him. He was carrying a racing form, as he had been at the racetrack before going to Logan Airport, I guess to calm his mind and submerge in the puzzle of trying to pick a couple of winners. He looked so handsome decked out in grey pants, white tennis shoes and a red-and-white striped shirt, worn outside his pants. We embraced briefly and held hands walking together to the lounge. We sat at a small table, our knees lightly touching, while having a beer as we waited for his luggage. We engaged in some small talk, mostly about not believing we were actually together after five months apart.

We didn't actually kiss for real until we got in the car (maybe subliminally we thought someone was watching us at the airport). When he reached across in the car to kiss me, I felt like I was in heaven (what a kiss!). Then he kissed me again (what a doozie!). We drove as fast as we could to the Embassy Suites.

I recall John's tennis shoes squeaked as we approached the front desk. I felt myself glowing and to the desk clerk we must have looked like two high school kids checking in to a hotel after prom night. It was like we were two giant neon signs flashing *WE ARE IN A HURRY!*

After getting our room key, John asked the bellboy to carry his suitcase up to the room, which I thought was a little odd. When we got to the room, the bellboy showed us how the curtains opened (who cares?). Then he received his tip and left us alone for the first time since March.

It was at that point that John turned to me and held me in a soft embrace. Then he kissed me gently and he said, "Are you ready for me?" Well, that was just about the sexiest thing anybody's ever said to me. But what was I expecting, for him to throw me on the bed and rip my clothes off (well, maybe)?

It was the best couple of days of my life as I encountered experiences that I never thought would ever happen to me. We made love, showered together; he even washed my hair. Is this what love was supposed to feel like? If it was, I was definitely missing out on it. Along with romantic evenings eating in our room, watching movies like *Casablanca*, and playing Trivial Pursuit (for some strange reason I always beat him in the medical categories), we also went out to dinner and even found time to play miniature golf (I think he let me win). Some evenings we would stroll around a local park, holding hands like teenagers as we walked. One time we visited Lake

Minnetonka and had a drink at a little place called Mai-Tai's as we watched the sun sparkle on the water. My life in Rochester was only 80 miles away; but it felt like 800.

I know it sounds like a cliché, but it is true; all good things must come to an end. But it was no less heartbreaking. We checked out and went to the airport and said our goodbyes. I waited there until I saw the plane move away and then went out to the car and cried. At that time I didn't know that next month we'd be together again, at the same hotel, more comfortable with ourselves than we had ever been before.

While together we'd rarely ever spoke about what we were doing or of our spouses, but he did tell me that he felt so at ease with me because his wife was very modest in the bedroom.

Except for Marianne, no one knew about our time together. But my oldest daughter, who was 20 at the time, looking back at that moment, recently said to me, "I just remember, Mom, that you smiled so much more and you looked like you were so much happier?" I guess she was happy for me, too.

For me, it was a thrill of a lifetime and I wish everybody could have felt as I did in that airport hotel we dubbed our

Shangri-La. And when John's letter arrived a few days later, I knew that he felt the same way I did.

My Dearest, Dearest Connie,

I love you more than I ever felt it possible to love another person. Thank you so very, very much for the most wonderful time I ever had in my life. I miss you more than I ever thought possible. I love you more than words will ever be able to say. Everything reminds me of you. All my dreams are of you. I just have this aching and longing for you. I can't help it. It hurts like hell. When will I see you again?

I love you more than my life. Forever, John

John & Connie

Minnesota, August 1987

The first time together since Orlando

Little Darlin's
Rock N Roll
Palace
Kissimmee,
Florida

Where it all

began...

1987

1995

2001

2002

2005

2010

2018

Chapter 6

A Marriage on the Rocks

Our much-anticipated and utterly enjoyable meeting in Minnesota in August only fueled our desire to be together always. Even before checking into the Embassy Suites, before an evening of cuddling while watching *Casablanca*, and before beating John at mini-golf (though I have my suspicions he let me win), the wheels were already turning on bringing my marriage to Jack to a screeching halt.

That June, I had approached Jack about a divorce. His reaction was predictably neutral; as if I had just asked him what he wanted for dinner. There was no yelling, no screaming, no accusations. I felt I had done everything I could to save a marriage I really didn't want to save, even to the point of visiting a marriage counselor with Jack. And this was unusual for him because Jack was the kind of guy that didn't think anybody needed a psychologist or psychiatrist or any help for something that you could do yourself. But he went. And all I could think was we're here to make a separation easier. To make a divorce easier. Because when the only feedback you are getting is, "You were a mediocre lover anyway," it's time to pull the plug on a marriage barely surviving on life support.

The time spent in Bloomington with John only accelerated moving in that direction. I wanted Jack to be out of the house as soon as possible. And I think it took him another two months to face reality, and another two—October—to actually move out. But looking back on that summer—for all its highs with John— it was also a very uncomfortable time in the Thamert household.

Could the kids sense it? Perhaps, at least Rachel, who was 20 at the time, might have felt the bad vibes. And when I came out and said that I met this person who lives in Boston, my son, Mike, who was 18 at the time, said, "I think that's too soon." Mike was that kind of guy.

But I was certain of one thing; I knew I didn't want to be with Jack anymore. So when the divorce became final on December 12th, it felt like the weight of the world had been lifted from my shoulders.

Strangely enough, although we were both involved in very unsatisfying marriages, throughout all our letters, and phone calls, and time spent face-to-face, we never bad-mouthed each other's spouses, and certainly never used the "d" word in our conversations. But John could tell by the tone of my letters or the inflection in my voice over the phone if I had a particularly bad day at home. He knew when I was upset. Still, while he was raising my spirits, I also knew he was battling the same fight as I was back in Boston.

At one point that summer he told me that he had gone to visit his parents who lived in Braintree, a suburb south of Boston. He tried to bring up the fact that things weren't so great at home. And he said that Rosie, his mother, would have none of that kind of talk. She brought up something that happened 15 years prior as the reason, stating that it was all his fault. He wasn't getting any support from his mother. Then he said his son and his sister both called him and they were giving him a hard time. I felt really bad he had to go through all that. And sometimes it seemed like we were the only two people on an island.

Marianne certainly knew that things were going downhill fast at home, as did a friend at work and Jody, another friend of mine. On John's end, a few people knew about it, including the guys that were with him on the Orlando trip, and his oldest son, John, Jr., who got us a price break on the hotel.

After asking for a divorce, and our first meeting in Minnesota, we did a lot more phone calls and a little less letter writing. I would still put dinner on the table and then say I had to go to a meeting, which meant there was a phone call that I was going to make. My daughter, Rachel, would drop me off and pick me up, none the wiser. I know John wrote his letters at his desk, and used his office phone to make his calls. He never wrote letters from home. After all, I was such an honest and nice person (my nickname in college was "Honest Con"), that nobody would have ever conceived that I was in the throes of a hot and passionate love affair with a man far, far away. Maybe that's why I got away with it so much. I can remember mentioning to John in a letter how I felt.

Yes, dear one, you make sense, at least I understand it, about having to spend time with a person I'd rather not be with. But that someone is still here, and that's not even fair. But my pretending, however, is over. Yet, I really can't spend all the time I'd want talking with someone I'd rather be with. Maybe someday. That's all I'm hoping for right now.

Still, another milestone was set to unfold. After our two rendezvous in Minnesota, it would be my turn to reciprocate and journey east to Massachusetts, where in November John and I would share some time together on beautiful Cape Cod.

Hello my Dearest Irish Sailor,

It's so hard being so far away. It can be lonely. Sometimes I feel you are so alone and I feel so inadequate over the phone. I'd give anything to spend more time with you. I am so looking forward to getting to know you better, I told a friend about our plans and she said, 'Oh, I'd love to see Cape Cod in November.'

Waking up next to you is the most comforting, beautiful and exciting experience in the world. To awaken and reach out and to touch you. When I am with you it feels like I have always been with you. I miss you so very much. I must close now, darling.

Missing you, loving you.

Love always, your Con

Chapter 7

Getting together in Massachusetts (Cape Cod & Boston)

"If you're fond of sand dunes and salty air
Quaint little villages here and there
You're sure to fall in love with old Cape Cod"

By November of 1987, Jack had moved out of the house and the divorce proceedings were chugging along, although at times it seemed to be at a glacial pace. The kids were doing pretty well and just a few people knew what had been going on since that night in Orlando some eight months prior. Still, I wasn't ready to climb on the roof and shout out to the world that I fell in love with a married man at a Denny's in Central Florida.

So, when John and I discussed that this would be a good time to have me reciprocate the two visits he had made in Minnesota, it was decided that Cape Cod in the fall was the place to keep our flame burning one-on-one. We decided that November 7th through the 11th would work best. As far as my family was concerned, I was off to one of those pesky, boring nurse's conferences in Boston.

John told me I would love Cape Cod, and that he had some great memories of the place. Plus, chances were miniscule that I would run into anybody I knew down there, especially in the off-season.

I knew even before the plane landed at Logan Airport that John had everything orchestrated in his mind. I would walk off the plane and not take off my sunglasses. And that first embrace wouldn't be a huge bear hug but simply a brush of a hand. And then barely a kiss on the cheek. The plan was to control ourselves before we hit Cloud Nine (and before you think what you're thinking; Cloud Nine was the name of the lounge at the airport). We sat and had a drink and then went to get the luggage.

The first night we stayed at the Logan Hilton, with a plan the next day to journey north to Concord, MA to check out Thoreau's Walden Pond. From there we headed south to Cape Cod and checked in at the Blue Water Resort. It was very quiet on The Cape that time of year, with many businesses closed for the season. But we soaked up the solitude, choosing to lounge in our large hot tub while drinking Harvey Wallbangers. Other days we would just sit and stare at the ocean. As mentioned previously, John loved the water, and I had only seen the Atlantic Ocean once before, on a prior business trip to Atlantic City. John would point at the buoys bobbing in the water, and explain to me how they are used to help ships with their navigation. We saw a mother and daughter walking along the beach, and even named a seagull, Sophie.

We had dinner at a wonderful little restaurant called Captain Parkers, did some shopping at the Cape Cod Mall, and even had time to watch the dog races before it was, sadly, time to journey back to Minnesota.

In a letter to John, I couldn't help but think back on what a great time we had on Cape Cod.

My Dearest John,

I just read the part of your letter that felt like we were still at the Blue Water on The Cape. I can't write through tears either. What a lovely place. Our time, our pool, our whirlpool, our restaurant (practically) for breakfast, our beach, our boardwalk, our deck, our seagull Sophie, our guitar players, our Harvey Wallbangers, our mirrors to take pictures in, our lovemaking, our steps down to the ocean, our spot to watch the ocean, our miniature golf course, our lovely showers, our caring words, our buoys, our Cape Cod. Our wonderful caring, our wonderful sharing, our wonderful Blue Water. Oh, darling... our love.

Do you realize how much we shared at Blue Water? Maybe more than most people share in a year. And it was only two days. We can make it, my dear... I know we can. And you know it, too. Like you once said, 'Something as wonderful as our love for one another doesn't come easy. But we must endure.' So we will, my love, so we will.

I look forward with all my heart, with all my soul, with all my mind, all my being to January 8, when I will see you again.

Love always, forever and a day. Your sweet and gentle lily, Connie Faye.

Even though we had planned to meet in Boston in January, it was a sad farewell as we knew the holidays—which always seem to magnify emotions, both good and bad—would be coming up with us 1300 miles apart. We did exchange Christmas presents—I bought him a jacket (I put notes in all the pockets) and he bought me a Claddagh ring (he kissed it before sending it to me). January 8th, the planned date of our next rendezvous, seemed light years away.

In the end we survived being apart for the holidays, as hard as it was to endure. Although the pain was mitigated to a degree by my divorce to Jack becoming finalized. I had also made the decision to tell my children that I met someone special while I was at the "Nurses Conference" in Boston, to which they seemed to be okay with. Things were starting to speed up.

When I returned to Boston in January (I told the kids I was going to see John), we stayed at the Marriott hotel on a deal John's son worked out. It was a short trip—just a couple of days—but we made the best of our time together. We even went to the horse races at Suffolk Downs.

Because of the divorce being final, and the cat pretty much out of the bag, this trip, if it were possible, felt happier and more relaxed. We had a great time. We would tease each other relentlessly, which I guess I never felt comfortable teasing my first husband because he wasn't much fun to tease. I mean he wouldn't get it. And I think John had the same problem with his marriage. She would get angry at him if he teased her. So when we started teasing each other, it was just perfect.

While in Boston he finally showed me where he worked, and where all my letters had landed throughout the year.

This was the trip where we also knew that our situation could no longer continue as it had. It was wrong and very unhealthy that two people who felt so much for each other should be separated by a time zone. The pieces were now in place to—as they say in racing jargon—to cross that finish line. I knew it, and I knew John knew it, too.

Dearest Connie Faye, My Darling,

Well, babe, things have started on their way to us being together. Not a giant step, but perhaps a crawl, or even getting up on your knees to crawl. But however you wish to describe it; they have started to move in that direction.

I love you, Connie Faye. To know you is to love you. To not be with you is to miss you terribly. To wake up beside you is heaven. I love you so.

Your rattlesnake and only yours, John

P.S... we WILL be together, my love.

And I needed to let him know I felt the same way.

My Dearest John,

I want to start my life with you and your life with me. Our life together. What a lovely thought! To be able to love you without missing you. To provide comfort to you. To give you all the love I possibly can. Yes, John, darling, you will always be my endless love. Our lives have just begun. I could never resist you, my dear heart, and never would want to. You mean the world to me.

You and I shall be home. We will have come home, so very, very soon.

I love you more than ever before. All my love to you, your Connie Faye.

Smile, sweetheart smile; we are coming home to each other, to be together always.

The die was cast and there was no turning back from where our hearts were leading us. That path had been long but it was a journey we would gladly make again. Still, the best lay ahead of us. And 1988 was shaping up to be a landmark year for John Rohanna and Connie Faye Thamert.

John's lifelong motto,
"Just one more!"

Quiet time in a park after
love pulled us together,
permanently, turning our
distance apart from 1,330
miles to 0 miles.

John's favorite spot in the world, relaxing on our deck, enjoying time with our dog, Freckles.

Quick with a smile and a laugh, blessed with friends and family

Can you tell by our expressions who the winner in golf was?

71

At the 19th hole on the deck after a round of golf at
one of our favorite getaways, at Madden's Golf Resort,
Brainerd, MN.

Here's to happiness at Annie and JW's wedding, knowing like us, they were coming home.

At our home golf course of Meadow Lakes in Rochester, MN, hanging with so many friends and family. Only John could make turning 70 so much fun!!!

Enjoying $1 martinis after a round of golf...just what the doctor ordered to relieve body aches at McGuire's Irish Pub in Pensacola, FL.

Modeling John's favorite scally cap during Shangri-La 1.

Enjoying a moment in nature next to Walden Pond during Shangri-La 3 in Concord, MA.

Chapter 8

Love *After* the Pages

After almost nine months of constant letter writing, clandestine phone calls, and secret motel rendezvous, things were starting to come to a boil. With every turn of a page of the calendar it was becoming more and more difficult to be apart, even though we knew if we made the ultimate decision that there would surely be some personal collateral damage.

We had discussed the possibility of John moving out to Minnesota and being with me even before the end of 1987. But there was still some trepidation and a sense of needing to feel like this was the right decision, no matter what the blowback would be. John addressed his concerns in a letter he sent to me on January 4, 1988.

Hello, My Dearest Connie Faye,

I want you to think about what we talked about today. About all the ramifications my coming to live with you would mean. Think about what problems I would bring you and also what problems I would cause you. I know I have spoken with you about this but I want you to give it a lot of thought. Once things are set in motion here, they probably will be unstoppable. I love you- so I don't want to be the cause of unhappiness for you, but I DO WANT US TO BE TOGETHER. But I want you to be 100% sure. I AM.

I love you and always will no matter what you decide. I love you so.

Your Rattlesnake, John

I had absolutely no doubt what I wanted to happen. My divorce was final and Jack had moved out. Rachel and Annie seemed okay with my meeting "another man" (my 11-year old, Annie, asked if we made it to '4th base' Once I figured out what she meant I then had to figure out why an 11-year old knew to ask about 4th base). My son, Michael, wasn't terribly thrilled, but I was hoping he'd come around.

On the east coast, John was dealing with some drama of his own. There was a blow up at his house following our January get-together in Boston that made his young daughter, Shauna, cry (she was his favorite). And it was around then that his father's sister died. Still, I think at that time he had told at least two friends and I think his son, John, the oldest one, that he was going to move to Minnesota. Even at this point, I don't believe he had told his wife that he was leaving.

Once the decision was made that John would move out to Minnesota, wheels had to be put in motion, some of it dependent on his business, which he had pretty much decided to walk away from. Business was always slow in the winter, so the timing was right. But I know he left inventory enough to cover the phone bill, which was pretty high considering all the "507" area code additions.

When I returned from my Boston visit on January 10, I told the kids that John was coming to visit. Remember now, they thought we first met in November, having no prior knowledge of what had transpired during the eight months before then. The girls were fine with it, but Michael, then 18, remained silent. I asked Mike if he thought he'd like to meet John. He said, "I don't know." It turns out Annie would be with her dad in Faribault at that time. I told her John and I would still meet her for sure and she thought that would be a great idea.

I suggested to John that he stay at my house, but he thought it might be less awkward if he just stayed at a motel. I wasn't sure I agreed, the feeling being if we are going to take the plunge let's just jump right into the deep end of the pool. But in the end I bent to his wishes. And maybe he was right. John rented a motel room on February 13, outside the city next to a nice restaurant called John Barleycorn's.

The plan was that we would have dinner at my mom's, which would also include Rachel and her boyfriend. I can tell you that morning John was more nervous than a squirrel at a dog park. The day started out precariously as the Minnesota winter took its toll on our car battery parked outside the motel room where John and I stayed. Eventually we got the car started and then went to my mom's. Now, my mother was a little Spitfire, and only stood about five feet tall. And when I told her we had a problem with the car and it wouldn't start, she said "Well, that's what you get for catting around." It was so perfect. And she and John got along great. Rachel was very happy for me and we had a great dinner.

After dinner, Rachel and her boyfriend, Joel, and John and I, went to a bar and played pool. Ironically, the name of the bar was "Cheers." Very appropriate. We hung out with them and had a good time and they both really liked John. Now there were still two more kids for John to meet.

Michael was staying at our house and we chose not to stop over right away because I didn't want to get Michael more upset and he had made himself scarce. Maybe he went to his dad's house, about 60 miles away. And while I was staying at the motel with John, Annie stayed with her dad on the weekend and then she was over at her girlfriend's house. And that's where she first met John. She seemed to like him, but it's not always easy to read an 11-year old girl. Sadly, on this particular visit John would not meet Michael.

On this visit we finalized the plans to have John leave his life in Massachusetts and move to Minnesota. To say this was a giant step in our relationship would be an understatement. The logistics were that I would fly to Boston in mid-March and we would drive back to Minnesota together. Ironically, that would mark the one-year anniversary of when we first met in Orlando; a whirlwind 12 months to be sure.

In March I met John at Logan Airport and we stayed that night at a motel. The next day we left. He had already packed up his little Toyota Corolla wagon. It was a lot of stuff. Mostly he had garbage bags full of books, more books than clothes, which really didn't matter. I think his wife went to work so he dropped Shauna off at school. And that tore at his heart because she didn't know that he was leaving. He never told her, and I scolded him for that. I said you should sit down and talk to your kids. I mean, at least tell them. If they hate you, they hate you, but they deserve to know. I have no doubt that when we drove out to Minnesota from Boston he was dealing with some guilty feelings. Not all the baggage was sitting in the back seat of his Toyota. I think he felt the weight of the judgment of his family bearing down on him. He felt everybody was against him doing what he did. Plus, he was worried about getting denied visitation rights with his children. He also told me his wife thought he would try to take the children to Minnesota. John would never push for that.

We tried to make the best of the three-day trip to Minnesota. We stopped in Ohio to eat at a place called the Rathskellar. But the funniest thing was we stayed at a motel where you can park right outside the door to your room. We were in such a hurry to get into the room after six hours in a car, we didn't even take out our luggage and instead bolted into the room like two horny teenagers. A few hours later we emerged from our bliss only to find we left our car doors open. Fortunately, some highly literate thief didn't steal John's garbage bags full of books.

As for living arrangements, it was also determined that our days spent living in motels would come to an end and that John would move in with me. I wasn't going to have him move all the way here and live in an apartment. I didn't see the point in that. And as far as I was concerned, we were together and we would always be together. And that's just how I looked at it. I guess I felt a twinge of guilt because Annie, my 11-year old, was still living in the house, but it didn't really bother me that we weren't married because I knew that we belonged together.

Michael was another issue. He had just broken up with his girlfriend of a couple of years and of course he wasn't in any state of mind to be reasoned with. I mean, nobody was ever yelling or anything like that. But progress between Michael and John was slow, although eventually it all worked out. Maybe you could call it a truce. Strangely, Marianne, who was more or less the catalyst for all that was happening, kind of disappeared off the grid. I don't know if I ever did anything that upset her. In the end, I think she kind of liked the drama of what had been going on for the past year. And once John was here, it didn't interest her a whole lot.

Now I know what you must be thinking. After all we had gone through in the past year, we must already be on our way to see the Justice of the Peace and tie the knot. But interestingly enough, John would not have the divorce finalized with his wife for another five years. To be honest, I guess it did bother me a little. We talked a lot about it, and maybe there was that one thing I didn't like about him and that was he could procrastinate a bit, and I'm not that way. But I knew eventually it was going to happen.

Let me explain a bit more why I didn't push John into the divorce by nagging him or criticizing him. I found the most effective way to get him to do something distasteful was to encourage him. He contacted his old friend, George Madden, after years of not being in touch and said it was due to my encouragement. We were both pretty stubborn so when he reconnected with George, he credited it to my encouragement. So I also tried to get him to sit down and tell his kids about what was going on so they didn't blame themselves somehow. But I knew he couldn't do that; he hated confrontation. So when it came to divorce, I supported him in doing it his way and in his time. When he got called back to Boston to take care of some business, it was probably better that he wasn't in the middle of divorce proceedings, and he could see his children without that going on. He stayed with his dad. The matter of divorce wasn't a priority at that point. I was patient (for once in my life) because I knew he would get to it and if it made his visits to Shauna's soccer games more enjoyable and not confrontational, it made things easier somehow. After all, we had probably missed out on the first 25 years, and knew it wasn't going to be easy. I guess we did the best we could. Still, the best was yet to come.

I think I summed up my feeling best in the last letter I wrote John on February 24, 1988, just after he had met my family.

My Dearest John,

Remember to look forward to our living together. Remember what a beautiful word together is. Your Connie Faye wants to be with you more than anything in the world. I will always stand by you. I will always be with you. If people want one of us, they get both of us. Ah, yes, we will have our problems, everyone does. But we can see them through. I know we can.

I want to share moments of joy with you. Together. I want to share moments of tenderness with you. Together. I want to share moments of passion with you. Together. John dear, we do all these things so well. We are especially good in bed (Oh dear, I don't believe I just said that!). I want to look in your eyes, it's like a 'fix' I need. I want to share a laugh. I want to share a wink. I want to share a joke. I want to share a tear. I want to share a kiss. I want to share a hug. I want to share my life.

We were meant to be together. Somehow it has been planned and is meant to be. I love your craggy, Irish face. I want to look at it when I want to, forever and a day. We will appreciate all we have been given. We must nurture our love like a precious flower, with leaves so soft and petals so smooth, always providing nurturing soil. We must never turn away from the other's love. It would be like a flower turning away from the sun.

We must take the time to bask in the sunshine of each other's love, and then the flower of our love can grow and bloom larger and fuller.

I love you, my John Rohanna. Don't forget the love I have for you. There are no doubts for me and no doubts for you. As long as we have each other, we will be ok.

Remember, my darling, how I do love you. I will never leave you. Never. You are stuck with me standing by you all the time. I am missing you terribly, aching for you. Soon, loving you <u>without</u> missing you will be wonderful.

Love always, Connie Faye

USED CARS • LAND • WHISKEY • MANURE
FLYSWATTERS • RACING FORMS • BONGOS

John & Connie

"SEEKERS OF FUN & ADVENTURE"

(507) 288-2597

WARS FOUGHT • REVOLUTIONS STARTED
ASSASSINATIONS PLOTTED • BARS EMPTIED • TIGERS TAMED
UPRISINGS QUELLED • AND - BARS TENDED

Chapter 9

One Big Happy Family

On March 15, 1988, almost a year of long-distance foreplay, and maybe one or two white lies, came to a halt. That was the day John Anthony Rohanna (formerly of Boston) moved into the house in Rochester, Minnesota that I once occupied with my first husband, Jack. Our household now consisted of 12-year old Annie, who always got along well with John, my 18-year old son, Michael, who at best had set up a truce with John. My oldest, Rachel, who was 20, was away at college in Mankato. I think John made a big difference in Annie's life. I think she needed somebody like him or she just needed more, maybe more discipline than she got from her dad and me too, probably. But Michael wasn't too interested in that. The two of them often eyed each other warily, like lions protecting the same lioness (me).

So a legitimate question might be, "Did it feel weird to me?" Truth be told; it felt right to me and I make no apologies to anyone for his being there, because it felt so good. I would have done anything to have him here. We had a great time from March to the following January. John wasn't working so we spent a lot of time watching TV (lots of golf), maybe drinking a little too much, went out to some restaurants, and just generally enjoyed each other's company. And during that period we really never discussed money, or if John should get a job. I don't know how much he brought with him. I mean, he could have sold three cars and it was all cash business that he handled. He always had money, but he didn't have to pay rent. He didn't have to pay for food. I took care of that until he started working.

It was also during that time that we discussed selling the house (which I received in the divorce proceedings) the following year. But there were some things that John had to attend to beforehand. In January 1989, he flew back to Boston to be with his dad because his mother had died of throat cancer. He stayed with his dad because he felt he really needed him, and I certainly didn't object. And at one point I flew out there to meet his dad and his sister and, and his older two kids, and that felt a little strange. John stayed in Boston until September of 1989, although he did come back briefly in June and July.

Once John was back for good in Rochester, we started to put pieces in play to sell the old house. And I think a good part of the reason was we wanted to live in a house that felt like *our* house. Besides, I was only working part-time (although making good money as a nurse) and really couldn't afford to stay in the house as the interest rate was something like 11.5% back in those days, and I knew it would keep going up. So we bought a new house a few miles from the old one.

That would be our home for the next 30 years; 30 wonderful years. John would eventually get a series of jobs; working for an auto repair shop, working at Wal-Mart, but I never pressured him. I could appreciate how hard it must have been for a man of 50 years to suddenly uproot his life and say goodbye to his kids and friends and move halfway across the country.

Our life felt like a storybook. We'd sit in the afternoon on the deck and have a few beers, maybe watch golf on TV. We never really argued. I only remember one disagreement we ever had in our life and I can't remember what it was about. But we got over it and got through it, whatever it was, whatever we had argued about. But there was one other time when John and I had a disappointment. We had traveled to Boston to attend his oldest son's 40th birthday party. John Jr. had wanted his dad to be there but was put in a tough spot because his dad's second wife was uncomfortable with my attending. When John Jr. called his dad, I could see John was getting really upset by what his son was proposing. He was saying, "You and Connie can come and stay for a little while, and I will have you go out the back door. " This would take place before John's second wife showed up. But my John would have none of that. So instead of going to the party, we went out to dinner and had a nice time. Interestingly enough, when John Jr.'s brother, Tom, celebrated his birthday the following year, their mother, John's first wife, insisted we both attend which we did.

As the years went on, I would eventually run into John's second wife at family events, but I don't think over the 30 years I spoke 12 words to her, mostly along the lines of "You have beautiful children." I recall when their daughter, Tara, got married and I was in the procession line, which was nice, because I got to meet a lot of John's friends "from the old neighborhood." I remember somebody that day asking me why I didn't take John's last name, and I replied, "I thought there were enough Mrs. Rohanna's in the world." And then I said,

"Will the real Mrs. John Rohanna stand up now?" It was just a joke, but they all liked it.

Speaking of weddings, after five years of "playing house," we got married on March 6, 1993. Rachel was my maid of honor, and John, Jr. the best man. We got married at a little chapel in Las Vegas. The Justice of the Peace was named Richards, and I believe his claim to fame was he once performed the ceremony for Richard Gere. I thought that was pretty cool.

We spent a lot of time with my friend Jody and her partner, Jerry. We played a lot of golf at some great courses all around the country. We golfed in Florida, Alabama, Colorado, Iowa,

Wisconsin, and many courses in Minnesota. Rochester had three municipal courses that we belonged to and there was a course called Meadow Lakes (not one of the city courses). Meadow Lakes was open from 1997-2012, and if you joined ($3,000 for a couple per year) green fees and carts were covered. Many friendships were developed on those courses. One special friend for John was a little Italian guy named Cozzy from New York. (Yes! A Yankee fan of all things!). They gave each other such crap but were very good friends. Anyone who ever golfed with them remembers the occasion with much humor. No one drank during play- but they didn't need it to keep up the insults. Then, of course, there was the 19th hole- on the deck of Meadow Lakes Golf Club, which was always fun. Then every other year starting in 2001, we went to Myrtle Beach with a group of 12 friends for six days of golf and fun. John Rohanna was never a great golfer, but NO ONE had more fun golfing than John!

It was strange; I don't know if Jack ever had friends. If asked me what Jack was really like, I wouldn't be able to tell you. I guess Jack was the kind of guy that would become your friend and he could be good friend, but he would become your friend because you knew how to play tennis. And he wanted to learn how to play tennis. It seemed he always wanted something out of the friendship.

Eventually John and Jack would meet for the first time. It was at Rachel's wedding and it was the funniest feeling because we met in a church and it was like meeting an insurance salesman. He said, "Hi, Connie, it's nice to see you." And shook my hand, I was expecting him to hand me his business card. But they were civilized to each other.

Another great trip was going to Denver for a wedding, as that was where Rachel had moved to. We went to a lot of race tracks, including Saratoga. And at one point I said let's go to the Kentucky Derby. But he would not even go to the local race track on the Kentucky Derby day because it would be too crowded. He didn't want to fight the crowds.

John always said I had a "lilt" in my voice (no one has ever said that before or since). He compared my voice to a lullaby and always said it was like "sleigh bells in the snow.' Even in the last years, when I would call him from work, he would always say it was his pleasure to listen to "sleigh bells in the snow." He said that every time. How lucky can one woman get?

But even the best storybook has a final page, and our storybook closed on April 16, 2019, when my John passed away after a long illness brought on by cardiac amyloidosis. It's when the protein leaves your bones and deposits itself in your heart. And these little cells deposit between the muscle cells. And eventually you die of heart failure. Usually people will get that in their 60's. So maybe living until his 80's was because he was happy and we were happy together. That is a nice thought. And maybe also because I am a nurse and I needed to take care of him at the end. Still, there were times when that was very difficult.

I became ill on April 2 and had to have a friend drive me to the Emergency Room. It was two in the morning and I left without telling John because I didn't want to upset him. I called Annie and she called hospice and they arranged for John to go into the same hospital where I was having gallbladder surgery.

We both came home on April 8th, but I couldn't care for John at that point, so Annie and her husband stayed with us. Her husband, John Wilson, was a godsend and actually changed my dressings, made sure John got from the bed to the chair (I could lift nothing), made him soups and encouraged him to eat. He even made sure John would stand up every couple of hours. My John was fading awfully fast, but even then he insisted on meeting me in hallway to kiss me goodnight, until he no longer could. He died eight days after we both got home.

Annie was the closest John and I ever came to having our own child. She and her husband, John (who we called JW), did so very much to help us through that trying time. They were always there for both of us. And God bless Hospice; what a help it was to have those nurses be there.

We held hands a lot during those final days; tough days. It felt appropriate since holding hands had been our thing ever since that night in the car on the way to Denny's on the Ides of March. After John passed away I went through some of his belongings and found the business card I wrote my information on that morning in Denny's, and the key to the Embassy Suites where we had our first rendezvous. That touched me so that he held on to those for all those years.

After John died, I went back and reread all those letters we had written to each other, over 300 handwritten letters of unwavering love. Today, the originals are filed away by month in a plastic file box in a closet. The good copies are in plastic sleeves (each page in one) and in three-ring binders (labeled month by month), and the binders are in order by month in my living room on the bottom shelf of entertainment center. Then I have copies in brown envelopes labeled by month, and these are "loaned out" as needed to anyone that is interested. One person reading them is a dear nurse friend that I told in October of 1987 about what was going on. The other is my daughter Rachel, who has just started reading them. Annie has read some and promised to read them all before she dies.

So we close. But I would be remiss in not mentioning the letter that John wrote to me, his last letter, as he battled his illness. How appropriate that a relationship that was borne of letter-writing should be given such a beautiful finale.

To My Beloved Wife.

We used to ask a question when we were writing; what has more meaning, the spoken word or the written word? I don't know the answer, but I have these words, and now I will write them.

I must tell you how much I appreciate you being my Beloved Wife. Your support means so much to me during these trying times. I feel guilty putting you thru this. Your love keeps me going. I am so lucky to have had you as my lover, wife, and best friend. You are a fine, wonderful, caring person and again I am so blessed to have you in my life.

Churches have their way of making saints. But in my mind and God's eyes, you are a saint.

Your Everlasting and Blessed Husband, John

Thank you for being you.

Never letting go at our last Christmas together 2018.

John and my daughter, Annie

John and my oldest, Rachel

John & his son, Tom

John & John, Jr.

John, Annie & her husband, John

Arlington Race Track, Chicago… 2014

Me, John & Annie's husband, John

John at the National Naval Museum, Florida, with his beloved USS Saratoga (2014)

Chapter 10

Final Thoughts

John and I spent much time and wrote many lines in our letters wondering just *how* did this happen, and *why* did this happen?

We ended up knowing each other for 32 years, one month and one day, and being married 26 years. We anticipated some big revelation, but it turned out to be the GIVING OF LOVE to each other, and that was reason enough.

I believe he described what we had perfectly in a letter he sent me on his 49th birthday, September 22, 1987.

Con,

You said in a letter that you hope I would never let you push me around. Well, Dearest, I think that just reverts back to what I just said. You would never push me around nor I you because THAT would not be giving love. It would be taking, and neither one of us would ever want to do that I know. Nor do I think either one of us would have or will ever take the other for granted. Our moments together - be they by letter, telephone, or in person, are too few and precious for either of us to take the other for granted, and even if we did- That would not be giving love again, and our gift is too beautiful and precious to ruin it.

It is our responsibility to continue to give love. Giving love nourishes the gift. It makes it so very strong. The more love we give to each other, the stronger it becomes. Someday it could be like the Rock of Gibraltar, but if we take love, we take from our gift and eventually our gift would weaken and die, and it is too beautiful to ever, ever let that happen. It would be a Sin to do that, my Gentle One. A Sin.

Looking back I ask myself, "Would his heart failure had struck him sooner without this love he received and gave?" Perhaps. But more importantly, I was there beside him to care for him and give him all my strength and love that I could.

And if I could write one more letter to John, it would sound like this:

To my John,

I thought of you today; not once or twice, but every few moments it seemed the memory of you came to mind. I felt you today; you are beside me always, and not only beside me but inside me as well. The image of you is engraved upon my

104

mind and my heart. I never ask myself if this is love. I know it is. I never wonder if I am complete. I know I am.

You made me whole by your caring, your understanding, your love. And in all my thoughts of you, I feel the joy of our togetherness, the security and warmth of the knowledge of our love. I am truly blessed. Forever and a day.

Your Connie Faye

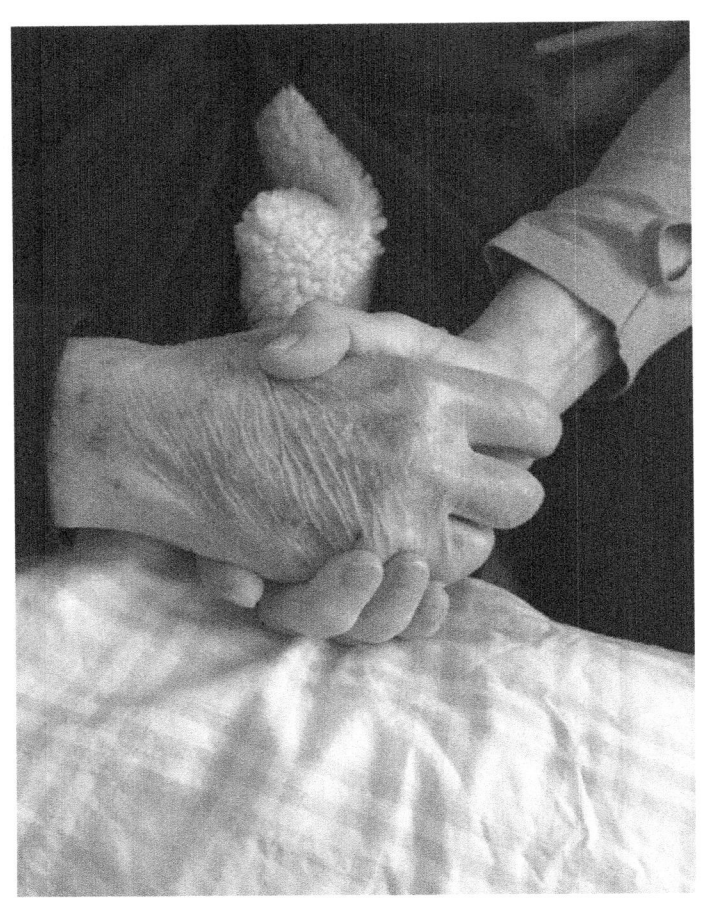

John "Roey" Rohanna passed on peacefully Tuesday, April 16th, 2019 at home surrounded by love. John was born in Boston, MA, on September 22nd, 1938, to Anthony & Roselle (Roche) Rohanna. John lived much of his life in Boston, but moved to MN to marry Connie Thamert, his wife of 26 years, who survives him. He is also survived by, his sister Diane Jackson, children John Jr. Rohanna (Haydee), Thomas Rohanna, Dennis Rohanna, Tara Fitzgerald (Scott), Shauna Rohanna, eight grandchildren, a niece, a nephew, three step-children, Rachel Gordon (Scott), Michael Thamert (Megan), Anne Wilson (JW), six step-grandchildren, plus several grand dogs (including Fang).

John enjoyed reading very much, with special interest in WWII Naval History. John proudly served in the United States Navy (1956-1958, 1962) on the USS Saratoga and had a frightening front row seat during the Cuban Missile Crisis.

John enjoyed sports immensely. He was an avid fan of the Patriots and the Red Sox. He talked often of his younger days going to watch the Red Sox play in Fenway Park. He was also very passionate about horseracing, having owned a racehorse, and enjoyed many hours handicapping races. John could study racing forms, watch races, and usually come up with a mortal lock to win. Some did, some didn't, but he was right in the saddle on every race. His greatest enjoyment may have been golf, where Roey made the greatest friendships over the years. Watching and playing, golf was always interesting to him. He was very competitive in golf and always found himself involved in wagering, side-bets, a smooth cigar on the 10th hole, and sidesplitting laughter. John played in many Rochester All-City Golf events, taking home his share of hardware, and he always competed to the last hole. Even if there was no trophy won, or money made, the real joy and happiness came in the comradery he had while playing. Often the round was replayed many times at the 19th hole with family, friends, and competition. Not many, who ever played golf, went to the track, or watched any kind of sport with John, ever left not having a great story to share any time they got together. John will be missed by so many.

A heartfelt thank you to Mayo Hospice and all those who served John.

A celebration of life memorial will be hosted on Saturday, June 1st at Eastwood Golf Club, 3505 Eastwood Road SE, Rochester, MN 55901, including an optional round of golf and a gathering with food and drink at the 19th hole afterwards. Times TBD.

The life we shared

Our favorite song

Greenfields of France

Somewhere Out There

Our favorite movie

Airplane

Our favorite TV show

Moonlighting

The Black List

Our favorite beverage

Vodka & tonic

Our favorite place to visit

Madden's Resort (Brainerd, MN)

Our favorite thing to do on a nice day

Golf and sit on our deck with friends

Our favorite thing to do on a rainy day

Meet friends at Happy Hour

Our favorite food

Steak or prime rib

Our favorite restaurant

Michael's

Papa George's

Our favorite holiday

John's birthday

Our favorite sports team

New England Patriots

The one place we always wanted to go but never got there

Ireland

Our one great regret

We didn't meet sooner

Our nicknames for each other

Him: Tootsie, My Irish Sailor

Me: Angel in White, Lily of the Springtime

Our favorite author

Lee Child

Our favorite season

Golf Season

Our guilty pleasure

Veal Parmesan

Made in the USA
Monee, IL
17 June 2021

71598855R00066